ORGANIC BATH

Make All Natural Bath Bomb,

Body Butter & Body Scrubs

16 Natural Recipes

By

Molly Barrett

CSB Academy Publishing Co.

P. O. Box 966

Semmes, Alabama 36575, USA

Cover Design & Layout

By

Robin Hamilton

First Edition

WHAT'S INSIDE THIS BOOK

INTRODUCTION

ARE you the type of person who's serious about feeding your family organic meals?

Do you make special trips to the different area grocery stores and local farm markets to ensure that everything your family eats is free of carcinogens and other health-threatening synthetic substances?

That's great! So why do you settle for buying bath products for your family that are loaded with additives that are known to potentially cause health problems, raise the odds of you and your family members eventually develop serious diseases, illnesses and disorders?

You've probably been aware of this problem for some time, but until now weren't sure what would be the best method of handling it. After all, it wasn't until quite recently that the manufacturers, the Food and Drug Administration and other government agencies are acknowledging this problem.

That's only after Europe has known about this situation for literally decades and made great strides to amend it and make their citizens not only feel safer but, in fact, ensure they are safe when using commercially made bath products and other cosmetics.

Up until now, you've really been held captive. If you want clean skin, there wasn't much on the shelves of the bath and beauty shops to choose from.

What if I told you that it's now easier than ever to bypass those synthetic ingredients and the very real possibility of adverse side effects?

And what if I told you that it costs less than what you're currently spending on commercially made bath products and is more satisfying to use than you could ever imagine?

Would you be interested?

There's a solution that more organic-minded families are discovering every day. And more people than ever are using. They're making their own custom-crafted bath products.

Before you dismiss this without giving it any thought, you need to know that it takes practically no time at all to make any of the three products I mentioned in this book. I'm also willing to bet that with the exception of just a few items, you already have all the ingredients for these products in your home.

Now, you're ready to listen. Let's talk about three of the most popular (and most luxurious) categories of bath products first: **Bath Bombs**, those fizzy balls of love and healing you toss in the tub when you're taking a soothing bath, **Body Butter**, and **Body Scrub**.

How can I be so confident that you'll find these artisan items more appealing than those sitting in bath shops across the country right now?

Because several years ago, I was where you stand right now. Looking back I call it my fork-in-the-road moment. It was the moment I decided to take action against what I had been railing about and take on, in my own small way, the giant manufacturers of these products.

No, I didn't protest at their factories or sue them for potential health concerns. I just quietly gathered all the ingredients I needed to ensure that with these three products, I would never have to use a store bought product again.

Today I make all the body bombs my family uses – and I give even more away as gifts. And so many of my friends have been so supportive I'm even considering selling them at local craft festivals and online. Oh, I'm not out to earn a fistful of money with these products, although you could very easily. No, for me, it's more about ensuring that consumers are aware of the possible dangers of store bought ones.

I also make body butter for just about every member of the family and body scrubs, or exfoliates, that slough off extra dead skin cells and allow the new ones to grow healthier and more radiant.

This book is a result of my friends begging me to put my expertise and my recipes on paper. My very first book DIY Natural Melt and Pour Soap Crafting was my first try and now here is the second one. But it's also an integral part of my journey. I share these with you because of my intention that every family should have an alternative to bath products that may have less-than-healthy ingredients.

This is not to say that my journey is yours. You may find that the activities in this book will bring you and your children together as you work side by side not only making awesome organic bath products but also making memories that will last a lifetime.

It may also be that you've discovered a journey of creating a side income, which ultimately, improves your self-confidence and teaches you lessons you never even knew you needed to learn.

Whatever path that creating your own customized organic bath products take you, rest assured at the end of the day, you'll be more satisfied than ever and more assured of that you have taken at least a few of the potential health-damaging ingredients at bay.

So let's get started!

CHAPTER 1: MAKING ORGANIC BATH BOMBS

BATH bombs are without a doubt miraculous. One of nature's better creations I dare say. You can choose from a nearly endless array of colors, from pastels to darker colors, shapes (who said they all had to be round) and sizes. When it comes to the bath bombs, one size does not fit all.

Bath bombs can be described in one word: **Magic**.

Well, maybe they aren't quite magic. But you can't deny they work magic on your body.

The truth of the matter is that bath bombs, regardless of the size, scent or shape are derived from mundane materials. What's even more disappointing to the daydreamer in us is that a bath bomb is nothing more than the result of a chemical reaction. There's nothing magic or romantic about that!

Every bath bomb – homemade or commercially manufactured -- has the same base elements. The fizzing action is the result of a combination of acids and bases reacting to each other, while a powdered ingredient acts as a filler. Lastly, a binding agent works to keep everything packed together. It is up to the "creator" of the bomb (that's about to be you in a moment) to choose the aromatics, colorants and other additives.

Interested in being a modern-day alchemist, turning chemicals into magical items?

If you're interested in making your own organic bath bombs consider the following to see what's involved. And now, you don't need to wear your wizard's hat and cloak. You really don't even need that wand you're holding.

Now that you've put down the wand read the list of ingredients you'll need to create this magical experience perfect for every member of your family. You may already have many of these ingredients in your kitchen cabinets. If you don't, you'll want to buy them before you start your first project.

BAKING SODA

Yes, we're talking boring old baking soda. The same baking soda you place in your refrigerator to draw out unpleasant odors. This is, without a doubt, one of the two critical ingredients in creating this magical experience of bath bombs. It, combined with the citric acid, put the fizz in your bomb, causing it to explode the moment you hold it under the bathtub's faucet.

When you think of baking soda, you may also think of those small boxes them. You can buy it in these small containers, but if you believe you're going to making these bath products often, think about purchasing larger containers of them. The largest I've seen so far is a thirteen and half-pound bag of it. But, I wouldn't be surprised if you can't find this in an even larger bag.

You may have a bit of trouble finding citric acid lying around your kitchen unless you can fruits and vegetables. Go to the canning section of your grocery store or any hobby store to buy this. It's the other part of the reaction with the baking soda that puts that fizz in your bomb.

COLORS AND SCENTS

We're going to talk more about the types of dyes and scents that are safe and gentle on your skin. Before you go shopping for your ingredients, you'll probably want to read that section.

One thing to keep in mind is that you're making *organic* bath bombs. This usually assumes that you'll want to avoid adding commercial dyes – which are easily found in craft stores. Instead, steer yourself into the natural section of your favorite craft store.

The same idea prevails when you're searching for the right types of scents. You have your choice among several categories. But you certainly don't want to buy any fragrance oils. These are commercial grade scents and potentially contain the harmful ingredients you're trying to avoid when you make organic bath bombs.

You may want to choose from an array of **essential oils**, but in a later chapter, we will discuss your options. You'll discover a whole new world opening up to your olfactory senses.

REMEMBER THE CORN STARCH

It seems like a letdown to go from talking about all the ways you can make your bomb an explosion of color and scents and then tell you that another boring ingredient, in addition to your baking soda, is needed to make your bomb.

Cornstarch. I told you it was boring. But as boring as it appears, it plays a marvelously enhancing role in your product. If you've used bath bombs before, then you recall with delight the amazing silky feeling they leave with you.

Start to thank cornstarch for the feeling. It may not seem possible, but it is.

OIL

As with the dyes and scents, there are so many options at your disposal. These oils also come in a wide variety of prices. Before you decide on one or choose a recipe with one, double check the price and your budget.

You have at your fingertips, almond, coconut, argan, olive oil and even buckthorn oil. Any of these choices will obviously soothe and refresh your skin, but they'll also moisturize it as well.

LIQUIDS

While water works just fine, you can also upgrade your product by adding rose-petal water. Rose-petal water is usually the first choice of those who have sensitive or dry skin.

SALT

Salt?

Yes, you can add ordinary household salt when the recipe asks for this or . . .

You can add something a bit more upscale. My guess is you'll probably go upscale. Why not try Epsom salts? Not only will this ingredient take some of the pain out of your sore muscles, but they'll also pull the toxins from your body.

THE EQUIPMENT

Making bath bombs is so simple that the list of equipment you need for this activity is embarrassingly short. You can use your hands when you mix the ingredients, and you can even shape them into bombs with the use of any mold.

You will, however, need a measuring cup.

Eventually, you'll probably want to buy several molds. We all do it. And there's nothing wrong with that, especially if you want to give these marvelous bath accessories away as gifts.

You may also want to get, once you're making these for craft shows (they are easy to market and practically sell themselves) a digital scale. In this way, you know that each ball is roughly the same size. It's essential to know this if you ever of think about selling them.

LOOKING FOR FIZZ IN ALL THE WRONG PLACES?

When it comes to making a bath bomb, you can use any skin safe acid and base combination in order to get the fizzy bubbles. However, the classic tried, tested, and the true organic combination is baking soda and citric acid.

If you're wondering how much of each to use. Your chances of having a great bomb is when you begin putting your recipe together using the following ratio: two parts baking soda and one part citric acid. The base and acid combo need to make up at least sixty to ninety percent of your total bath bomb recipe.

POWDERED INGREDIENTS

You can use your discretion whether you want to add and how much you'd like to any powdered ingredients – like the following listed below – in your bath bombs. Many add the various powders because they can improve the texture and enhance the healing and relaxing benefits of the bombs.

If you believe you want to try them, don't stick to the ones below. Once you become adept and confident in this hobby, you'll find that any type of powder that's safe on the skin can be used in the bomb. The ones I've listed below are just the most common and most loved ones.

➢ Milk Powders

➢ Salts

➢ Starches

➢ Clays

➢ Honey Powder

- ➢ Grain Powders

- ➢ Herb Powders

As you can see, even the few noted here are capable of changing and enhancing the ultimate appeal of a bath bomb. And once you move from novice to veteran, you'll discover that if you can imagine a bath bomb with just about any particular powder or powders. Then, it's not hard to make at all.

Just so you know: Your powdered elements can account for nearly 40 percent of the bomb itself.

There are, however, two substances that you will want to keep out of your bath bombs, for safety reasons. The first is **Borax**. If this substance should, by chance gets consumed, it can damage your kidneys and liver.

Similarly, **corn flour**, which adds a refreshing soft texture to your bath water and soothing on your skin **but** can all too easily trigger yeast infections.

COLORS AND SCENTS

Ah! Now we're talking about the core experience of the bath bomb. For as much as it's a delight to your skin, much of the bomb experience is about color and scent and especially the healing and restorative qualities your body – and soul – receive in this luxurious type of bath.

CHAPTER 2: COLOR YOUR WORLD AND MUCH MORE!

TO be truthful, I've heard more than one person say that choosing colors for the bombs is the part of the process they enjoy most. They feel like a kid again in art class.

You certainly don't want to miss out on this fun. So, don't suddenly get frugal when you're faced with this decision: the colors, if any, of your bath bombs. The beauty of the bomb is in its ability to accept and look spectacular whether you use a water-based or an oil-dispersible coloring. Just remember as you begin, that each category is used differently.

Water-based dyes are more than likely liquid. This means you add them to your water-based binding agents. Additionally, this type of dye can also be added to any of your powdered components simply by using a bit of salt. All you need to do is to dye the salts or the binding agents before putting them into your recipe.

On the other hand, the liquid or powdered oil-dispersible colorants – this would include oxides, micas even D&C dyes – can be put into the oil-based binding agents or even mixed other powdered ingredients.

The amount of colorant you add to your bath bomb recipe can be adjusted based on the yield you want for a specific shade of color. Just keep in mind that using too much colorant can result in your skin and the bath fixtures changing colors. If you aren't sure, always start out using less than what you want. Then you can stand back and judge what you have.

I know many people who use commercial grade dyes – D &C and FD&C. But if you're not familiar with these you may not realize that basically they're synthetic dyes – not strictly organic. The initials D&C mean that the Food and Drug Administration has declared these colorants safe to be used in drugs and cosmetics.

That's what the initials stand for. FD&C dyes, in addition to the latter two uses, can be safely added to food as well.

It's true that both of these categories of dyes will provide bright, bold and beautiful color to the bomb and the bath. But you may want to think twice (or three times) before using them.

They aren't necessarily organic. And most people enjoy making bombs knowing that they're adding natural substances to their bath water.

The other disadvantage of using this category of dye is that it fades and bleeds with time. So, as beautiful as they are the day you make them, you'll find some of their charm fades over time.

Instead of these, why not consider **Micas and Oxides**. These two types of colorants are less likely to bleed. You can also choose to use naturally colored powdered ingredients for a truly organic bath bomb by adding things like clays and herbs.

Mica

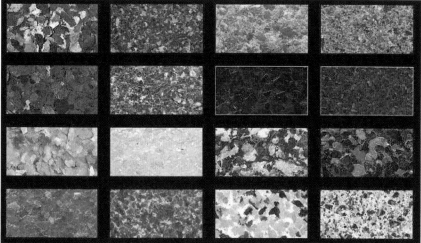

Mica Color Chart

MICAS AND OXIDES

Oxides are pigments that are made in laboratory. They are regulated enough to be considered safe to use in beauty products On the other hand micas are actually natural organic products in the earth, however, cosmetic grade micas are not.

Cosmetic grade micas are synthetically produced in a lab, like pigments, and have been since the 1960s. Cosmetic grade micas are the same stuff you see in your lipstick, eye shadow and blush or other mineral makeup.

Oxide

AROMATICS

Choosing just the right scent or better yet blend of scents for your bath accessory offers you versatility in your choices, but a great time as well. Most people choose to use fragrance oils and essential oils for this purpose.

I prefer essential oils over the fragrance oils. And I'll tell you my biggest reason. Just as with the colorants, fragrance oils are considered a commercial grade scent. If I'm paying meticulous attention to ensure that all my other ingredients are organic, I don't want to risk any type of potentially harmful side effects.

Essential oils from Buff & Butter

But, you may want to consider scenting your bomb using absolutes, attars or even CO2 extracts. But more than that, if you're looking for just a light scent, you can enlist the help of an aromatic binding agent, such as a Hydrosol or Floral Water – both of which we talk about in a bit more detail later in this book.

Searching for a natural scent? Then you'll want to experiment with aromatic oils and butter. Think cocoa butter, organic virgin coconut cream oil for this. When you add these, you'll discover the result is a delicious subtle scent that draws you into the tub.

When you use scents, you may discover that you, indeed, can get too much of a good thing. The number one rule (in fact, it might be the only rule, to tell you the truth), is never use more essential or fragrance oil that is safe for a single bath.

And how would you know how much is 'just right"?

Your aromatics should never be more than _one to five percent of your overall total of your bath bomb recipe._ A little does go a long way.

ATTARS

We made a passing reference to this method of creating a scent for your bomb a few paragraphs earlier. Attars, if you've never heard of them before, they are traditional Indian perfume oils. They were created only for the use of perfume artisans who took their craft seriously.

Indian Attars

Originally, they were distilled from flowers, roots, spices, and herbs and placed on a base of sandalwood oil. This may not sound like a painstaking process, but to get the proper aromas, sometimes this meant three months of distillation – just sitting in the base waiting for the right time, much like a fine wine in the West.

There were even certain scents that demanded a slower process. It wasn't unusual for some of these aromatics to sit for up to several years before they yield their finest scent. The result was a complex, rich aroma.

The sandalwood oil base, in effect, was used as a fixative, a substance that extends the herbs and other items in the oil, peak aroma for as long as possible.

Attars, as you might guess are unique. They possess a rich blend that is more than likely impossible by using only essential oils

Even today, after thousands of years, attars are still produced through a pure steam distillation craftsmanship process that ensures that the longer they sit, the better and richer the ultimate compelling, complex aroma.

You'll want to be careful though and use attars sparingly. Ensure that before adding more drops, believing the scent isn't quite right, allow it to blend and to cure.

Now a days, lot of on and offline retailers sell attars, but before ordering online, visit a local craft or body bath store to try some of the aromas of the attars this way there are no surprises.

HYDROSOLS

You would think those would be enough options for methods to scent your bath bombs. But, no. Wait, there are more. And one is them is call hydrosol. This is the pure, distillate water that's collected after an aromatic plant has been distilled through steam.

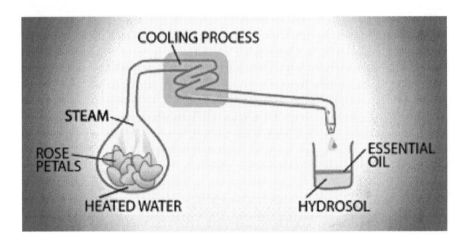

At times, you may have seen these referred to as hydrolats or distillate water. Whatever you call them you can be sure that they're not only clean but have the same consistency and appearance as water. Containing only a trace of essential oil, these are primary water-soluble aromatic compounds.

Hydrosols are perfect to use in toners, lotions, body sprays, room sprays as well as in creams. You can use these gently scented substances instead of plain water. The advantage of this is that you now have a natural aroma and beneficial effects all in one additive.

These are safer to use in any product that you may use as a facial than the traditional essential oils. You'd actually think, in fact, that they were made with those who have sensitive skin in mind. The one point to keep uppermost in your mind is that they need a suitable preservative to accompany them.

As you might have gathered from the above description hydrosols are actually more fragile than pure essential oils are. This means that they don't have the concentrated anti-microbial properties of the essential oils. This also means they can degenerate quite fast.

Even under the best of storage conditions the shelf life of these are as short as six months and certainly no more than two years. Their longevity depends first on the scent, believe it or not. If you decide to use hydrosols, then ensure that the following guidelines are met for optimum longevity.

Store these

- In dark glass bottles.

- Away from direct sunlight.

- In a cool, dark location.

- With the bottle caps tightly sealed.

Another important storage condition is that the bottle always stays as full as possible. If you have a large bottle of one, transfer it continually to smaller and smaller containers as you empty the containers.

No, this isn't due to some obsessive-compulsive condition I have. If there is too much "empty space" in the container, the oxygen will react with the hydrosol and cause oxidization. This, as you might suspect, only causes the scent to deteriorate even faster.

There's one more caveat when using hydrosols. Never allow non-sterilized items to come in contact with these substances. This includes your fingers or even cotton balls. Doing so will break down the integrity of the substance.

FLORAL WATERS

You've probably experienced the glorious light scents of floral waters without even knowing about it. These are water-soluble fragrances that are often used in linen sprays, facial and hair mists. In fact, if you have any scented water-based product, you are experiencing the magical scent of floral waters.

You may also find you enjoy these so much –and they are easy to use—that you'll be using them in place of water in your homemade creams and lotions as well. If you do, the same suggestions as I'm giving below apply.

There's absolutely no reason you can't use these in your bath bombs if you like. They're perfectly fine if you use them at their full strength. If, however, you find a certain scent a bit overwhelming, then you can always dilute them.

Lessening the strength of their aroma is certainly easy enough to do. Simply mix them with distilled water until you achieve the strength of the scent that you think appropriate for your bomb. Don't worry.

Adjusting the strength of floral waters is not an exact science. You don't have to worry about using a specific ratio. After you do find just the right scent, you may want to make a note of the ratio you did use.

Of course, it's not imperative, but if you ever want to duplicate that scent, it would make the process go easier and faster.

ACCESSORIES

Many who make bath bombs refer to the next category of ingredients as "additives." I prefer to call these items "accessories" because of the negative connotation the word "additives" has.

When I make any type of soap products, I see the word additives, and the first thought that comes to mind are commercial-grade, commercially manufactured items that contain health-threatening, possibly even disease-inducing substances. In a nutshell, I think of hidden substances that could very well damage your health, and that of your family without you even knowing they're tucked away in what you thought was a healthy product.

But by calling them accessories . . .

Well, now we're talking about a whole different category of items. And it's right here, with your choices you can set your gifts (your products if you decide to go into business) apart from the rest – and send them into the next level of delightfulness.

Think about the finishing touch for your bombs with engaging visual elements. When you think about this possibility, let your mind wander to how flower petals would look adorning your bombs. What about such items as herbs or sugar decorations?

Again, it's easy to do. In fact, there are two different methods you can follow. First, you can add them in with your powdered ingredients when you're mixing those. Or you can wait until you're almost done with creating the bomb and place them into the mold or if you're using your hands to make the bombs, press them on the surface when you form your balls.

BINDING AGENTS

A binding agent is that ingredient in your recipe that literally binds your powdered ingredients together, so they stay in a ball or the shape of the mold.

You can choose from two types of agents when creating these bombs – either work well. Regardless of the option, you decide on; the binding agent should compose only **ten to twenty percent** of your total recipe.

OIL-BASED BINDING AGENTS

If you're new to making bombs and are worried about adding water to your recipe for fear of setting off a premature chemical reaction, then investigate the possibility of using hard butter and oils. You have a choice of butter that would complement your bomb nicely, including _shea, cocoa or coconut oil_.

One of the aspects of butter you need to remember that as it cools, it hardens. You know this from the butter you use at home. If you keep it out of the refrigerator for several hours, it'll soften. But only an hour or so in your refrigerator and the butter has formed back into a solid again. It's the same concept with all types of butter.

Because of this, you may want to consider molding these individually. These would be the perfect bomb to shape by using ballers or various scoops.

There's one more thing to remember when using butter binding agents. And that is the Oil-based agents.

Bath bombs made with these binding agents tend to be softer and more fragile than those that contain water-based binding agents.

WATER-BASED BINDING AGENTS

Water is the catalyst in a bath bomb. That means that when your base and your acid come in contact with water, the fizz that we all wait for is created. That's why, if you plan to use a water-based binding agent, you need to be careful so it doesn't explode before it should.

At first, you may think that using water to bind all your ingredients is simply out of the question. But no, that's not true.

What is true, however, is that the final creation will be a harder bomb that is practically well . . . as one blogger called it "indestructible." Just how firm and tightly packed these bombs will be, though, depends on the other ingredients in the product as well as the technique you used to make it and the shape of your mold.

Some of my favorite water-based binders include hydrosol, floral waters or when all else fails, "plain" water. And here's a trick I use to get the bath product to dry faster: I add a bit of rubbing alcohol to it.

CHAPTER 3: TIPS, TRICKS, AND TECHNIQUES TO THE PERFECT BOMB

I T'S not at all unusual that, when you first started creating your recipes, forming the balls or using molds, that you're going to run into some, well let's just call them less-than-successful attempts.

It's that way when you try anything new, from a new recipe for dinner to learning how to knit or even writing a book. Who among us learned how to ride a two-wheeler bicycle without at least one or two falls or crashes? It simply comes with the territory.

So why should you think that making bath bombs is something you can just walk in on and do perfectly from the very beginning. No, I don't mean to discourage you from learning this satisfying hobby, I'm explaining that if your first attempt doesn't turn out the way you envisioned, don't give up.

This chapter is here to help you identify any problems that may crop up and explain why it may have occurred – so you can learn from the mistakes.

There's only one thing worse than making a mistake. And that's making a mistake and not knowing learning from it.

We all want to learn from our unsuccessful attempts regardless of the activity we're learning. And so here are a few tips, tricks and techniques to help you recover quickly when things don't work out the way you imagined it to.

1. The bath bombs are crumbling as you take them out of the molds.

If you find this happening to you, then they either need to be pressed together tighter as you put them in the mold or the mixture you used is too dry.

When you're placing your bomb into the mold, don't be afraid to press firmly. Another way to fix this problem is by allowing the bomb to stay in the mold for several minutes longer before removing.

If neither of these actions, "fixes" the problem, then your original mixture is on the dry side. Simply add a bit more water to your recipe.

2. Your bombs swell up into unrecognizable blobs.

This is the flip side of the previous problem.

Why does this happen? You guessed it. The mixture contains too much water or other liquid and your chemical actions – the fizz – begins. Don't panic and whatever you do, don't toss the mixture way.

You should be able to save this by adding more baking soda and more citric acid. Just be sure to add less water to the recipe the next time you make it.

3. The bombs are flat on the bottom

You may be able to repair this by ensuring that your bombs rest on crumbled tissue paper during the drying process. If you're pulling them out of molds when you discover this then allow them to dry for a couple of hours longer in there.

CHAPTER 4: BATH BOMB RECIPES

THE first step in making a bath bomb is to gather all your ingredients in one place, whether that's your kitchen table your counter.

Read your recipe thoroughly. Obviously, you don't need to memorize it, but you should have a handle on what's going to need to get done and when. Then prepare all of you ingredients individually. You'll want to, for example, combine all of your powdered ingredients – in the amounts indicated in the recipe – in one bowl.

Your next step is to create your binding agent. After that, you'll slowly add the binding agent to the powders as you continually stir these together. This keeps all the ingredients moving.

If you use and the oil-based agent then you only need to drizzle the liquid in slowly. If you chose a water-based agent, then you may want to add the agent by using a spray bottle.

You wet the mixture only a bit at a time. You know it's more than likely the right amount when your product has the consistency of snow.

Now that you've done this, you can begin the packing of the bombs into the mold or if you prefer to use a baller or a scoop to shape them.

The bath bombs should dry for three to six hours before you pack them away in airtight containers.

I'm sure you have at least a general idea of how the "building" of a bomb works, and you're ready no doubt and even eager to get on with it. Below, is a basic recipe to get you started.

THE BASIC RECIPE

Making organic bath bombs is all about choosing your own ingredients and making a customized bath experience for yourself, your family members and friends. In many ways, it can be considered an art. In other ways, it can be called a craft. However, you view it, the key to making totally delightful bombs is to enjoy the journey and the destination will take care of itself.

While you're traveling, don't forget to experiment until you find one you're totally satisfied with. At least for the moment. If you're like me, you'll probably never be done experimenting with colors, scents accessories and anything else that pops into our mind.

- 1 and 1/2 cups baking soda
- 1/2 cup citric acid powder (Found at your grocery store in the canning section)
- 2 teaspoons sweet almond oil
- Essential oil of your choice (3-5 drops)
- Coloring of your choice

Directions

Combine all dry ingredients in a bowl and mix well. Separately, mix the wet ingredients in a second bowl. You'll want to slowly introduce the wet ingredients to the dry ones.

As we've talked about, you'll want to be sure not to set off the "fizz" of the bomb. If you see a bit of the reaction occurring don't worry. Some will occur naturally, regardless of how slowly you put them together.

Your next step is to form the bomb into small bombs. You can either use a baller or you can place them into molds. If you want, you can also use a muffin pan as a mold. Take one of your pans and place a few drops of olive oil in each compartment.

This is, so the molds don't stick when they're done drying. Take the small balls you've formed and push them firmly into each compartment. You don't want to fill these cups too full because the bomb mixture will expand.

Make sure you store this in a well-ventilated location for a minimum of three hours or until they feel dry. If the atmosphere contains some humidity, you may need to dry them overnight.

Once you're satisfied, they are dried take them out of the mold and store them in an air-tight bag. Doing this prevents them from getting soggy. If you'd like, you can even use natural parchment paper store bags from your local health food store for this purpose.

MILKY ROSE BATH BOMB

With this recipe, you can make a truly wonderful floral scented bath bomb. Following the basic steps we've shown you above for the previous recipe using the following ingredients:

- 1 cup baking soda
- 1/2 cup citric acid
- 1/2 cup cornstarch
- 1/4 cup dry milk
- 3 tablespoons Epsom salt
- Handful of dried rose petals
- 1 teaspoon water
- 3-4 teaspoons Almond Oil
- 15-20 drops Rose Oil

Directions

Combine all dry ingredients in a bowl and mix well. Separately, mix the wet ingredients in a second bowl. You'll want to slowly introduce the wet ingredients to the dry ones.

As we've talked about, you'll want to be sure not to set off the "fizz" of the bomb. If you see a bit of the reaction occurring don't worry. Some will occur naturally, regardless of how slowly you put them together.

Your next step is to form the bomb into small bombs. You can either use a baller or you can place them into molds. If you want, you can also use a muffin pan as a mold. Take one of your pans and place a few drops of olive oil in each compartment.

This is, so the molds don't stick when they're done drying. Take the small balls you've formed and push them firmly into each compartment. You don't want to fill these cups too full because the bomb mixture will expand.

Make sure you store this in a well-ventilated location for a minimum of three hours or until they feel dry. If the atmosphere contains some humidity, you may need to dry them overnight.

COCONUT OATMEAL BATH BOMB

If you want a calming bath bomb that's great for sensitive or irritated skin then consider using the following ingredients:

- 1/4 cup crushed oatmeal (You can use a coffee grinder to crush the oatmeal)
- 1 cup baking soda
- 1/2 cup citric acid
- 1/2 cup sea salt
- 2-4 tablespoons Organic virgin coconut oil (In winter months use 4 Tbsp. oil)

Directions

Take the dry ingredients – the oatmeal, baking soda, citric acid and sea salt – and mix them in a bowl by themselves. Some people like to use a whisk for this step. It's important that you mix this well and make sure no lumps exist.

Next, you'll want to melt the coconut oil in a microwave or double boiler. If you choose the microwave, this step should take you no more than fifteen seconds.

If you're using a whisk, then take the whisk and slowly whisk the melted coconut oil into the dry ingredients bowl.

Once you've done this, then it's time to shape the bombs using a meatball maker. You'll want to wait a minute or so before you try to pop the bombs out.

Here is a great YouTube video on how to make this bath bomb, take a look

https://www.youtube.com/watch?v=Xuwoa6lzIQU

LAVENDER BATH BOMB

Nothing is more relaxing after a long, hard day than soaking in a bath scented with lavender. For a calming bath bomb, consider the following recipe:

- 1 cup baking soda
- 1/2 cup citric acid
- 1/2 cup cornstarch
- 3 tablespoons Epsom salt
- 2 teaspoons Sweet Almond oil
- 3/4 teaspoon water
- 17 drops Lavender Oil
- Dried Lavender Flowers (optional)

Directions

Mix together your baking soda, citric acid, cornstarch, Epson salt and the dried lavender herb. In another container place your almond oil, essential oil, and water.

Slowly pour the wet ingredients over the ones, carefully whisking them frequently until the two are fully combined. You can test to see if they are by pressing a handful of this batter in your hand. If the mixture doesn't hold, then lightly spray one or two spritzes of water to it. If you add too much, you'll ignite the bomb.

Once you have the right consistency, then put the mixture into the mold. Let it dry for at least two hours before testing to see if they're ready to come out. If they are, then place them on dry washcloths. Allow them to sit there overnight before packaging them.

EPSOM SALT BATH BOMB

Want to ease those sore muscles at the end of a day but not sure you want the lavender. Or perhaps you know a man who works hard who could use a surprise of muscle-relaxing fizz in his bath. Here is a recipe to try.

- 3 tablespoons Epsom salt
- 1/2 cup baking soda
- 1/4 cup cornstarch
- 1/4 cup citric acid
- ½ tbsp. water
- 1 tablespoon coconut oil
- Food grade coloring of your choice (optional)
- Essential oils of your choice (optional)

Directions

Place the following ingredients a bowl by themselves: baking soda, corn starch, citric acid and the Epsom salts. Whisk these together until they're well mixed.

In a separate bowl, add all the following wet ingredients water, essential oil, coconut, and food coloring. Add these wet ingredients in with the dry, slowly a bit at a time. Make sure you stir the mixture well between each addition of the liquid ingredients to prevent them from fizzing too early.

You'll know the two sets of ingredients are mixed well when it feels as if it has the consistency of wet sand. If this doesn't appear to be sticking well enough together to be able to form mold, then slowly stir in ½ teaspoon water in the mixture then stir well. Continue this until it does stick well.

Your next step is to pack half of the ornament with the mixture, making sure each half is filled completely. Press the two halve together and set aside. Do this until all the ornaments are filled.

Allow them to sit overnight. At this point slowly open each mold to remove it entirely from the bombs.

SINUS RELIEF BATH BOMB

No one enjoys being sick. If you get a cold or sinus infection, you want nothing more than to soak in a comfortably warm bath. You can also add a bath bomb to help improve your sinuses. For this you'll need the following ingredients:

- 1 cup baking soda
- 1/2 cup citric acid
- 1/2 cup cornstarch

- 3 tablespoons Epsom salt
- 2 tablespoons Sweet Almond oil (Pure)
- 10 drops Peppermint essential oil
- 25 drops Eucalyptus essential oil
- Coloring of your choice (optional)

Directions

Mix your baking soda, citric acid, and Epsom salts into a bowl and whisk together. Separately, whisk the almond oil, eucalyptus and peppermint essential oils as well the colorant of your choice in tint. Add the color slowly. It's amazing how little you'll discover you'll need.

Gently and slowly, add the oil to the dry ingredients.

Once you have the consistency you want, then scoop the mixture and press them firmly into your molds.

At this point, some people prefer to open the molds several minutes later to allow the moisture that got captured on initial closing to escape. Then allow them to sit for several hours until the mixture has set. Remove them and allow them to further dry overnight on dry towels. After that, store these in an air-tight container.

CHAPTER 5: BODY BUTTER

O F course, you love body butter, who doesn't? It natural moisturizing abilities along with its nourishing quality gives your skin a long-lasting and luxurious hydration.

And yes, we all know that body lotion can do the same thing (perhaps not as well). One of the differences that make body butter such a stand out in the bath and body areas is its distinct whipped texture. You begin to relax from your long, stress full day the moment the butter touches your skin.

The body butter is a very nourishing moisturizer that provides skin with long-lasting hydration. Its immediate difference from lotion is its distinct whipped texture. Let's first consider the differences between lotion and body butter.

For starters, some people spread it across all parts of their body; others only put it on their persistently dry problem areas.

If you're like me, you probably use it after your daily shower or bath when it can lock in your natural moisture for the day ahead. Of course, there's nothing wrong with using it after a relaxing evening dip in the bathtub when you can allow it just to soak in once you're in bed and allow it to do its best work while you sleep.

Come to think of it; there really is no bad time to use a good quality organic body butter.

Typically, body butter is made with cocoa butter, shea butter along with coconut oil and another vegetable-based oil.

You'll discover as soon as you place some in your hands that it's thicker than your average skin moisturizer.

WHAT MAKES BODY BUTTER DIFFERENT?

Both body butter and lotions are created with the intent of relieving dry skin and moisturizing your skin. Not surprisingly they also work in the same way.

So what's the difference between the two?

Believe it or not, the difference is the **type** of ingredients more than anything else.

The lotion is composed of a large amount of water, sometimes up to 70 percent water. This, of course, offers your skin an excellent moisturizing method.

The only problem with it is that it's only a temporary fix because water evaporates fast. This means that you find yourself applying more and re-applying the lotion as you feel your skin drying out.

Body butter, as the name implies, is made from a nut butter and essential oils. You might hear or see these ingredients referred to as humectants or emollient substances.

The difference is that it doesn't merely add moisture to your skin, but it locks it in as well. And when it does this, it also conditions and nourishes your skin.

Another difference, I'm sure you've already noticed is that body butter has a thicker texture than lotion. The more you use body butter, the more you'll see the amazing effects, and soon you'll end up with softer vibrant skin.

BENEFITS OF BODY BUTTER

Depending on your body's needs, there are an abundance of benefits to using body butter – especially organic body butter. Below, I've only listed four benefits . . . . that most people commonly need.

DEEP HYDRATION

We've already talked about this benefit –and it's one that just about every person needs – both women and men.

In essence, the long-lasting effects of body butter are because it creates a barrier between your skin and the outside world. Your skin, after all, is the largest organ of your body and at 22 square feet, it soaks in nearly 60 percent of what you and the rest of world put on it.

So, it's no small benefit that the body butter creates an effective barrier that can block at least some of the harsh, potentially health-threatening substances.

Not only this but regardless of the weather your skin will remain hydrate when you use body butter on a regular basis. Consider, in contrast, the use of lotion in its place. Lotion actually dries your skin. It encourages and enhances the evaporation of water in your skin. If you have extremely dry skin, there's no doubt about it; body butter is your best choice.

SKIN SOFTENER

When used after your shower, body butter can be an effective skin softener, thanks to the nut butter and essential oils.

PREVENTING CORNS AND CALLOUSES

If you suffer from corns and callouses, consider using body butter on these areas daily. This moisturizer can help to remove them. You should apply the butter after you've bathed and dried your skin.

Then you massage a small amount of butter into these areas. But, wait, you're not done yet. Then put thick socks on your feet. The following morning, you may discover that, using a callous scraper you can gently remove these irritants.

CHAPTER 6: MAKING ORGANIC BODY BUTTER

ONE way to think of body butter is as a super-concentrated body lotion. With less water and more butter and essential oils, its consistency is too thick to be pushed through a small squirt pump like some lotions are sold. It's much easier simply to scoop the butter out of jars.

And when you make your own organic butter, you'll find those who have sensitive skin will simply love it. Many times, the boy is made from cocoa butter along with organic shea butter and a variety of essential oils.

If you've never made it before, don't hesitate now to jump in and begin. It's easier than you think. And you'll be getting a hand-created butter specifically suited to your personal needs.

You're not surprised, I'm sure, to discover that different types of butter have different types of healing powers as well as various ways of soothing and moisturizing your skin. Here are just a few of the more common types of butter you can begin to consider using in your personal recipes.

SHEA BUTTER

Looking to reduce your wrinkles? Or perhaps just want to soothe that sunburn?

Then shea butter has your name written all over it. You'll also want to use this if you suffer from psoriasis or eczema.

And talk about healing qualities. The essential fatty acids found in this butter make it an excellent anti-inflammatory agent as well as endowing it with an abundance of antioxidant qualities.

Since it doesn't have a greasy residue or a strong scent, it's a popular ingredient in all varieties of body butter. Always keep in mind when you're making shea body butter that the ratio of solid to liquid will always be **75 percent to 25 percent (75:25).**

MANGO

Think of the mango. If you didn't already know, it's rich in both vitamins A and C. It also contains a wealth of fiber and potassium.

Each of these are excellent reasons to try making your own Mango body butter. But in addition to that mango butter is an effective cleanser for your pores.

COCONUT OIL

As healthful and healing as shea and mango butter are, coconut oil is just about universally considered as being even more beneficial to your skin.

It's legendary for its inflammatory and antibacterial properties and has been known to boost metabolism rates to help speed tissue repair. If that weren't enough, coconut oil is also regarded as an effective moisturizer and wrinkle reducer.

As we talked about and you've seen in the assortment of butter we've shown you, all body butter are natural moisturizers. But if you want a real increase in the benefits your butter, then turn to the essential oils.

We talked about them a good deal in the bath bomb section, but I'd be remiss if I didn't at least talk about one. It's the essential oil every other oil would love to be.

And that's lavender.

When you add lavender to your custom-crafted body butter, you've endowed it with a rich aroma that has therapeutic effects that can help with your managing stress and anxiety as well. Who couldn't use help in this area?

COCOA BUTTER

Cocoa butter is another hard-working ingredient you'll want to include in at least some of your recipes. From effective emollient properties to stimulation of collagen and elastin production, this is a must-try ingredient.

This butter also reduces the appearance of stretch marks and scars. And don't forget its amazing abilities to relieve the flare-ups of both dermatitis and eczema.

ALMOND OIL

You'll find almond oil as another addition to keep in mind for a body butter recipe. It can be extremely beneficial to your skin and your overall health.

Containing a rich amount of fatty acids needed to improve the skin's moisture barrier, almond oil is especially beneficial to those who suffer from itchiness and general irritation of eczema. This oil has an abundance of vitamin E, calcium, and magnesium.

All of this and a naturally light and calm scent in addition. If you've never considered this oil before, you may want to see how it can help your skin –and improve your health.

MANDARIN OIL

If you want to include antiseptic properties to your body butter, Mandarin oil is probably your best choice. Proven to stimulate both cell and tissue growth, this aromatherapeutic oil also aids in your overall relaxation.

Many people also think of it as an "anti-aging" oil. It's said that it puts the glow back into dull aging skin while fighting the formation of wrinkles. And it does all this with a wonderful orange fragrance.

OLIVE OIL

You've no doubt are well aware of the benefits of olive oil in your diet. Grilling with it, drizzling it over your salads. And generally using it instead of other oils. It's quite a legend when it comes to your health – especially heart health.

But you may not be aware of the same incredible health benefits this ancient oil brings to your skin. Yes! Your skin. It's a moisturizer like none other. If you have dry and sensitive skin and you've never used it before in body butter or other artisan bath products, you should see why people are raving about it.

Olive oil has also been known to help with the symptoms of skin cancer and sun damage.

But I want to add one word of caution about buying olive oil, make sure to buy from a reputable retailer as there are so many so-called "fake olive oil" sold in the market.

Hemp seed oil is the most versatile skin healer you can find. It stands out from the rest of the oils because of its high fatty acid content – it clocks in at nearly 80 percent.

It also contains nearly every amino acid we know about. So it shouldn't come as any surprise that it goes to work on your skin as an amazing anti-inflammatory agent and an effective antioxidant.

Believe it or not, the chemical make-up of this oils is eerily similar to that of human skin. Because of this, it absorbs into your skin without clogging your pores or leaving dealing with a greasy residue.

ALOE VERA

Aloe Vera gel is another ingredient you may want to consider to include in some of your body butter recipes. It works well to soothe sunburn, reduce skin inflammation as well as playing a vital role in an effective antioxidant.

But more than that, this natural gel helps with circulation and skin tissue repair. It's long been known to be a great cleanser for the digestive system. And if that isn't enough, it also contains 20 minerals, 12 vitamins, and 18 amino acids.

EQUIPMENT YOU WILL NEED

A DOUBLE BOILER

A good double boiler is essential to making body butter. A double boiler is essentially a pot inside another pot that holds and melts the ingredients when the outer pan/pot's water starts to boil, it, in turn, warms up the inside put and thus melting the butter.

Here is what a double boiler looks like. If you are on a tight budget, you don't have to buy one of these, instead just use two pots you already have in your home. A typical double boiler cost around $20-$35.

WIRE WHISK

A good stainless steel wire whisk becomes very handy when making and mixing body butter.

HANDHELD MIXER

For some recipes, you may have to use a handheld mixer, you will need either one that runs on electricity or one you turn by hand.

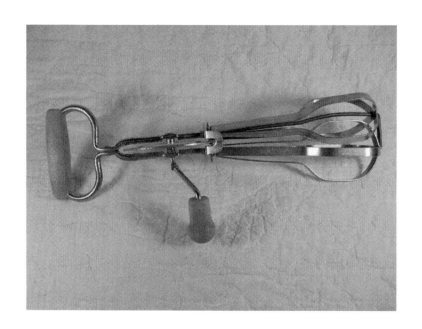

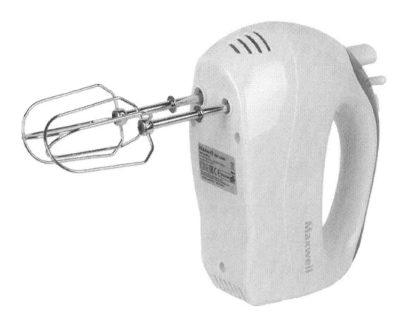

You will need some good quality glass jars that had good seals around the top so no moisture can get in and ruin your freshly made body butter.

MAKING BODY BUTTER

Here is a quick and simple description of how to make body butter. Once you have this routine down, you can make any type of butter whether you have a specific recipe or not. Remember there is no set rules or guidelines to make body butter, you decide, and you make the rule, and you create your own recipes.

Gather the ingredients you want to include in your customized body butter, put them in a double-boiler in which they can melt slowly without the fear of any scorching or burning occurs.

When the mixture is semi-clear you know, it's done. Refrigerate this mixture for several hours or until it's white and solid.

Take it out of the refrigerator and using a mixer, either an electric or a handheld, beat the oils until they are fluffy to appearance.

Add in the essential oils and beat the mixture again until they're thoroughly combined. Once they're fluffy, you can begin to transfer the body butter to jars.

And you'll want to refrigerate them for yet another hour.

CHAPTER 7: BODY BUTTER RECIPES

R IGHT about now, you've got to be scratching your head, wondering how something that feels so wickedly luxurious on your skin could be so easy to make.

And while I've never understood it myself, I still delight in it every time I use it. I have decided some mysteries of life are best left uncovered. The ease with which you can make it to the pleasure it gives you is one of them.

I've provided you with a few recipes to get you started. But honestly, by the time you've completed making them, you'll be experimenting with creating your own special ones. Guaranteed.

SIMPLE WHIPPED BODY BUTTER

Ingredients:

- 1 cup coconut oil
- 1 teaspoon vitamin E oil
- A few drops essential oil for fragrance

Directions:

Put all the ingredients into a large bowl. Don't melt the coconut oil, just place it in the bowl with the other ingredients. Mix all of this on high speed with a wire whisk for a minimum of six minutes or until the ingredients have assumed a light and airy consistency.

Spoon the body butter into a glass jar. Cover securely. Store it at room temperature or, if you'd like, you could refrigerate it. You may want to do the latter if you either live in a warmer climate or in summer.

VANILLA BODY BUTTER

Ingredients:

- 1 cup raw cocoa butter
- 1/2 cup sweet almond oil
- 1/2 cup coconut oil
- 1 vanilla bean

Directions:

Melt the cocoa butter and the coconut oil using a double-boiler. Remove these from the heat and let them cool for approximately half an hour.

In the meantime, grind your vanilla beans in a coffee grinder if you have one or a food processor. Then take the sweet almond oil and the ground vanilla beans and beat them into the oil mixture.

Place this batter into the freezer for approximately 20 minutes or until the oils begin to partially turn solid. At this point, remove this from the freezer and using an electric mixture of a food processor, whip it until it gets a butter-like consistency.

Now you're ready to spoon the butter into glass jars and store in a cool location.

Peppermint Body Butter

Ingredients:

1/2 cup coconut oil

1/2 cup cocoa butter

1/2 cup shea butter

1/2 cup sweet almond oil

1 teaspoon vitamin E oil

2 to 4 drops peppermint essential oil

Directions:

Heat the coconut oil, cocoa, and shea butter into a double-boiler. Stir occasionally to ensure the mixture is completely melted. Then you can remove it from the heat.

Stir in the sweet almond and peppermint oils and the vitamin E.

Place this in the refrigerator for approximately two hours. You want the mixture to firm some, but not get hard. Using an electric beater, mix beat this until it forms a whipped consistency.

Scoop the butter into jars. Store your butter at room temperature, and it will retain its qualities for six months to a year. Don't worry if it begins to melt; you can always re-chill it and whip it up again.

MANGO BODY BUTTER

Ingredients:

- 2 ounces cocoa butter
- 2 ounces mango butter
- 2 teaspoons shea butter
- 1 teaspoon wheat germ oil
- 1 teaspoon aloe vera gel

- 10 drops mango essential oil

Directions:

Using a double boiler, melt all the ingredient except for the essential oil. Stir this mixture occasionally until it's entirely melted.

Continue to heat if for another 15 to 20 minutes, until you're sure it's smooth and doesn't appear to have a granular consistency.

Once you're satisfied you have the right texture, remove this from the heat. Let it cool at room temperature. Once it has cooled, then you can add the mango essential oil into it.

Whip the body butter using an electric mixer until it's creamy.

Once creamy, you can pour into storage jars and keep at room temperature. This oil will remain effective for approximately six months depending on the storage conditions.

Hemp and Honey Body Butter

Ingredients:

- 3 tablespoons coconut butter
- 1 tablespoon beeswax
- 1 tablespoon honey
- 1 tablespoon sunflower oil
- 1 tablespoon castor oil
- 1 tablespoon hemp oil
- 10 drops desired essential oil

Directions:

Melt the coconut butter and the beeswax together. Then stir and continue to heat them for another fifteen minutes. In this way, the combination will not get grainy.

Add the honey and all the oils, except the essential oils. Stir this mixture until they're well mixed. Allow this to cool for ten minutes. At the end of the ten minutes, you can add your choice of essential oil or oils.

Transfer this into jars of your choice.

LAVENDER MANGO BODY BUTTER

Ingredients

- 1/2 cup Shea Butter
- 1/2 cup Mango Butter
- 1/2 cup Coconut Oil
- 1/2 cup light oil (like almond, jojoba or olive)
- Optional: 10-30 drops of Lavender oil

Directions

Except for the essential oils, bring this mixture to medium heat constantly stirring until the ingredients are completely melted. Remove this from the heat and allow it to cool for a bit. Now you can add any essential oils.

Following this, move this mixture to the refrigerator and allow it to cool in there for approximately an hour. You'll know when it's time to take it out because it will be just beginning to harden, but still be a bit soft.

Using a hand mixture, whip it for about ten minutes or until it turns fluffy. Return it the refrigerator for another 10 to 15 minutes to allow it to set.

Bring it out and pour the butter into glass jars with lids. Depending on how warm you keep your home, you may find that it made need to be stored in the refrigerator.

This is especially true during summers and areas in warmer climates.

Usually, this butter will get soft if exposed to any temperature higher than 75 degrees Fahrenheit.

SHEA BODY BUTTER

Ingredients

3/4 cup pure organic virgin coconut oil

¼ cup pure raw shea butter

3-5 drops essential oils (optional)

Directions

Mix the shea butter with the organic virgin coconut oil. Melt them together. Once well mixed add about three to five drops of essential oils of your choosing.

With a regular electric mixture. Once it takes on the smooth texture of creamy butter, you can then transfer it to a container of your choice at room temperature.

CHAPTER 8: BODY SCRUB

HAVE you ever enjoyed the luxury of using a body scrub? It seems ironic that even the savviest of those us who think we're taking the best care possible of our skin, probably haven't even thought of using a scrub on your entire body.

Sure, we've been using a body scrub on our faces for a long time, exfoliating to scrub off the dead skin to allow the skin glow as healthy skin should. But, what about the rest of your body?

Yes! When you exfoliate your entire body, your skin will not only have a smoother appearance but more than that, it'll appear re youthful. You'll look younger when you exfoliate your body regularly.

But those aren't the only reasons you may want to consider using a body scrub. When you scrub your skin, you not only slough out dead skin cells, but you're also increasing your body's circulation. Here are only a few benefits a good organic body scrub can improve your skin.

FRESH AND REJUVENATED SKIN

Hands down, body scrubs provide or skin with a fresh feeling and a rejuvenated and youthful look. The removal of the dead skin cells and their impurities allow the skin below it the chance to glow.

Consider this for a moment and then you'll know exactly why it's so crucial to exfoliate on a regular basis.

Science tells us that the human body sheds between 11,000 and 23,000 dead skin cells every hour. Yes, you use up to 23,000 skins cells every sixty minutes.

If that statistic seems to be mind-boggling, that's because it is remarkably hard to grasp.

SELF-TANNING

One of the little-known benefits of body scrubs is that they can help if you're trying to stay out of the sun, but you still want to look tan. They know the dangers of tanning and are trying to reduce their risk of skin cancer.

One of the ways some people are doing it – and they say that it's the best method – is through exfoliating your skin with a body scrub before applying any tanning lotion.

In this way, you're actively removing the most recent dead cells and allowing the newest portions of your skin to tan. Your tan last longer this way and the tan has a smoother appearance.

For all of the health benefits, many people don't body scrubs? Why wouldn't you? It seems like such a no-brainer.

Quite frankly, one of the reasons that body scrubs seem so luxurious is because they aren't most can afford on a regular basis. This is especially true if you want to buy an organic scrub.

I don't have to tell you because you already know how much money you could spend on scrubs. But when you make your own, you really can have your scrubs at still have some money left in your checking account.

Here's a quick look at what the initial costs of making your own organic body scrub. For a salt scrub, you can get an eight and a half pound from Bob's Red Mill for less than eight dollars. This yields about eleven jars of scrub that are comparable in size to that which you can buy in stores.

If you prefer the sugar scrub, you can visit any health food store and purchase Fair Trade organic sugar. You should be able to buy two pounds of this or around five dollars.

If you've already tried making the bath bombs or the body butter or both, then you already have the essential oils at home as well as the colorants, so that won't cost you much more.

At least, you'll be able to get yourself started.

CHAPTER 9: HOW TO MAKE NATURAL BODY SCRUB

CONGRATULATIONS! You've now made two of the three bath items in this book. I'm sure you had your doubts when you started. If you were confident you could do it, you may have been feeling a bit less confident of how long you would actually continue making these.

Sure, they looked fun and inviting at first, but you'd be denying human nature if at least a part of you didn't think at some point you'd lose interest.

But, honestly, you can see how difficult it is to lose interest in a hobby in which no two items you make are ever the same the products are not only useful but downright pampering.

When you reward is using these products, how could you ever stop?

You only have one more item to learn to make. Body Scrub.

I'll choose sugar . . .

No wait, I think I'll take the salt.

When you make your own customized body scrubs, you'll soon discover you have two choices as to what to use as the active exfoliating agent. You can either use sugar or salt.

So where do the differences come in?

Sugar scrubs, for the most part, are gentler on your skin. The sugar granules are round guaranteeing that they won't be quite as abrasive against the skin—but they still get the job done.

Sugar also dissolves faster thanks to the combination of it being exposed both to the hot water of your washing routine, but also from the heat of your skin. They'll disappear faster than salt does, so the granules have just enough time to perform their task before dissolving away.

While many argue that when you use sugar instead of salt, you're not getting the benefit of salt's natural mineral content. That may be true, but that's offset, others say, by the fact that a sugar scrub doesn't dry your skin out as a salt scrub does.

But that's not the end of the advantages of using sugar for your body scrub. Sugar's natural glycolic acid helps to make it an effective skin protective product. This acid helps both to condition your skin and moisturize it.

If you have sensitive skin, then you'll probably have to use sugar as your "go-to" exfoliate.

Salt Scrub: Can your Skin Handle It?

It's true that salt scrubs are harsher on your skin. If you were to look at a grain of salt and a sugar granule under a microscope, you'd immediately understand why.

Salt has sharper edges than sugar granules. While harsher, these sharp edges also smooth the rough areas of the skin better than sugar.

But even more than that, you may want to try salt scrubs for the therapeutic benefits and their mineral content. If you use sea salts, for example, you'll discover they are excellent at removing the toxins blocking your pores.

But wait . . . there are even more health reasons to use the salt scrub if your skin will tolerate it. For starters, salt exfoliating helps at boosting your circulation tightens your skin and overall salt scrubs help improve your skin texture.

You'd think that any one product that's as even half as beneficial as that would be difficult, intricate and complicated to make. Creating your own artisan body scrub is so easy to make.

Just check out a quick review of what's involved in the creation of every batch of body scrub, and you'll need no more convincing of making a batch or two yourself. It's the only way you can gauge for yourself the amazing benefits of this bath product.

You begin by pouring a cup of almond oil into a medium bowl. To this add a cup of sea salt or any other salt of your choice. Stir these two items together and any other items your recipe calls for.

Got it so far? Good. Because you got it. That's really all there is to it.

You only need now to transfer your scrub into dark glass jars with a tight-fitting lid. Yes, that's really all it takes. Now, let's discover what type of recipes are available to ignite your imagination.

You'll probably discover you're going to need more time to make a decision on which ingredients you use than the actual creation of the body scrub itself.

CHAPTER10: NATURAL BODY SCRUB RECIPES

FOR a natural sugar scrub use the following ingredients and use the general guidelines shown earlier to put it all together:

- 1 cup organic cane or brown sugar and 1/3 cup almond oil or olive oil.
    - *An alternative is a cinnamon and ginger sea salt scrub which contains the following*:
- 1 cup of sea salt
- 1/2 teaspoon of ground ginger
- 1/2 tablespoon of ground cinnamon
- 1 cup of almond oil or olive oil

BANANA SUGAR BODY SCRUB

This recipe solves two of your problems. What to do with those aging bananas and how to exfoliate and nourish your skin. Who knows?

When the bananas are starting to brown, grab those beauties and put them to use. This one skips the oil and relies purely on the benefit of banana and the gently abrasive sugar.

Ingredients

- 1 ripe banana

- 3 tablespoons granulated sugar
- ¼ teaspoon pure vanilla extract or your favorite essential oil (optional)

"Smash" the ingredients together with a fork. Yes, it is supposed to look like a gunky goop. But you don't want to "over mash" this mixture because you'll discover it gets too thin to be an effective scrub.

Want to use this on your face? Simply, reserve a portion of the banana and set it aside while you make the scrub.

Then mash it separately. But don't add sugar to it. When you're in the shower, use the sugar scrub to massage over your body.

But when you wash your face, use the banana-only portion and avoid getting it in your eyes. Then rinse it off using warm water.

Ingredients

- 1/2 cup baking soda
- 1/2 cup oatmeal
- 2 bags of green tea
- 1 cup of almond milk

Follow the general guidelines presented at the beginning of the body scrub chapter.

CRANBERRY BODY SCRUB

Ingredients

- 2 cups Imperial Sugar Extra Fine Granulated Sugar

- 1/2 cup coconut oil

- 12 drop essential orange oil or fragrance

- Airtight container or jar

- 1 cup whole frozen or fresh cranberries

Directions

Puree the cranberries, then add the coconut oil and sugar to it. Blend the items together. Add 12 drops of orange essential oil to the batter.

Once everything is mixed well, you'll scoop the scrub into air-tight storage jars and store it in the refrigerator.

CONCLUSION

ORGANIC bath products have always been in demand. But in the last few years, the focus of the consumers' interest has changed a bit. Perhaps your interest as well.

For years, the darling of organic bath products was homemade soap No longer can you say that with any confidence. Sure, these products will always have an attraction not only for consumers but also for those who create organic soaps simply for their family and friends.

Today, though, you see more people than ever before want more than the standard soap and body wash. Now there are wondrous, almost mystical organic bath products like bath bombs, body butter, and body scrubs.

All of these products have unique benefits and offer a wonderful cleansing experience.

There are two problems with commercially manufactured bath bombs, body butter and body scrubs, which in large part pushes this tremendous demand for though. The first is trusting the labels. When the label says "organic" what does that mean? The second is that the cost of these products has just "exploded" your budget right out of the water.

If you want a truly natural product a fraction of the retail cost, then consider making your own organic bath products. This book has just taken you, step by step on how you can do this.

Imagine being completely confident that the bath products you and your family are using really are organic and free of harsh additives that have been shown to be carcinogens and other health-damaging substances – many of which have already been banned in Europe.

Not only that, your family will think these items are expensive special treats (unless you tell them differently) and be thrilled to use effective artisan items.

LAST WORDS

I WANT to say THANK YOU for purchasing and reading this book. I really hope you got a lot out of it!

I am neither a professional writer nor an author, but rather a person who always had the passion for making and crafting beautiful soaps, body butter, bath bombs and body scrubs and since I have been making them for last 15 years now, I figured it is about time I share my knowledge with you, as I know there are many people who share the same passion and drive as I do.

Despite my best effort to make this book error free, if you happen to find any errors, I want to ask for your forgiveness ahead of time.

Just remember, my writing skills may not be best, but the knowledge I share here is pure and honest.

Can I ask you for a quick favor though?

If you enjoyed this book, I would really appreciate it if you could leave me a Review on Amazon.

I LOVE getting feedback from my wonderful readers, and reviews on Amazon really do make the difference.

I read all of my reviews and would love to hear your thoughts. If you rather give me a direct feedback feel free to email me at MollyBarrett2017@gmail.com

Thank you so much!!

Molly Barrett